INCLUDES THE RULES
FOR OVER 100 CLASSIC
CHILDHOOD GAMES

*RETRO*Active
Skip, Hop and You Don't Stop

GAMES WE PLAYED

D1114516

BY TOM O'LEARY

To Tim –

Whatever you do –

Remember to PLAY !

Tom O –

ISBN: 1-4392-5526-1
ISBN-13: 9781439255261

Visit www.booksurge.com to order additional copies.

DISCLAIMER: The author bear no responsibility for any injuries, accidents or other adverse consequences that may result from participating in any games listed in this book or any other form of play that this book might inspire.

Always be safe. Some of the games in this book were played in the street when the author was a boy. There are more cars on our roads today and it is extremely important to consider the safety of any area before playing there.

Vist us at www.gamesweplayed.com

Special **Thanks** to Clay Mountain, My big brother Dan, Big Rock, my sister (and Godmother) Cathy, the woods in front of our house, Annsville Creek, Uriah Hill basketball courts, sledding hill and field; Joe Koerner, the field, my sister Susan, the Assumption School courtyard, Continental Village, Terrence O'Driscoll, the Pump House, the iceberg incident, Lockwood Drive, Albert Road, my sister Bette, the streetlights that signaled it was time to go home, the patio, our backyard, my sister Nancy, the maple tree in our front yard, the willow tree, the ping-pong and ice hockey table in the basement, my brother Timmy, the snow, the rain, the sun, for never catching the cooties, for peanut butter and jelly, for lemonade, our Highland Park neighborhood in Peekskill, New York and to Mom and Dad for letting us be children when we were young.

✻ ✻ ✻

This book is lovlingly dedicated to my wife Dearbhla -- my three playful daughters; Meadbh, Aine and Aoife -- and the best dog in the world, Shadow.

INDEX

FOREWORD

Young Americans are in the midst of a health crisis. We cannot just sit back and watch their stress levels climb and fitness levels dive. More importantly, our children and grand-children cannot sit back any longer. They need to stand up, stretch out and get outside to play – and we need to encourage them to do so. It is this author's opinion that traditional play can help to address current stress and fitness issues and prevent future problems. Let's get our children in shape the old fashioned way – through play!

This book is a RetroActive guide for modern youth and a nostalgic look back at play for the parents and grandparents of children growing up in the twenty-first century. The author believes that by bringing childhood play back into our streets, courtyards, sidewalks and backyards; we can improve the mental, emotional and physical health of this and the next generation.

Sometimes, we develop complicated strategies to address basic problems. Many children in America are struggling to keep their weight under control. Others appear to be stressed out at a very young age. Since our traditional culture of play has changed over the past 30 years, we are seeing more and more children battling obesity. Is that a coincidence? I don't think so. Today, our children are all too happy sitting in the same spot for hours while engrossed by the electronic glow of a television or video game. When I was growing up, most children didn't sit still for five minutes when they could be playing a game outside.

When was the last time that you played *stickball? kick the can?* In eight short chapters, RetroActive brings back the memories of neighborhood play in the 1970s and 1980s; when communities were connected by the footprints of children. Including the rules for over 100 classic games requiring little more than the energy of youth and a ball; RetroActive takes a nostalgic look back at the art of coming together, making rules, picking "IT", selecting teams and most importantly *playing* in the streets, courtyards, porches, sidewalks, and backyards of our neighborhoods. I hope that this book revives the magic of play. I hope that it makes getting healthy fun again.

Now, **YOU'RE IT!**

With a playful heart and a sincere hope that children start playing again, the old-fashioned way!

RETRODUCTION

Every family in our neighborhood expected a knock at the door at some point on a Saturday morning. "Can Tommy come out to play?" some wide-eyed, knee-scraped boy would beckon. The only reason that anyone ever declined such and invitation was if they didn't have permission from their parents for some reason, and that was rare enough. When we were kids, play was our business. We took it seriously. We had rules. We spent every possible hour being with our friends and having fun. Our parents accepted that. They even supported it in a way. It was a mutually beneficial arrangement. They did big people things and we did little people things...in a big way!

We have advanced so much technologically since I played kick-the-can as a boy. Many games today require a connection to something and a power source. As much as I appreciate and enjoy the benefits of technology, I can't help but think that it has made us lazy in some ways. My grandfather used to walk to school each day; uphill both ways, barefoot in the snow (or so he said.)

Believe it or not, we actually had to get up from our seats to change the channel on the television set when I was growing up in New York. There were no remote controls, but we didn't mind. To be in control of the channels in those days meant moving to the television faster than anyone else. Survival of the fittest! We were happy to watch a program in its entirety - actually from the beginning to the end without flipping. But then, who wouldn't want to watch Welcome Back Kotter, The Jeffersons, Gilligans Island, Get Smart, Happy Days or Laverne and Shirley in its entirety? If the phone rang in the middle of the show we had to walk into the kitchen to answer it - standing there for all to see; whispering if we were talking about a girl, and definitely if we were talking to a girl!

Technology has obviously influenced the way we live today. It has influenced the way that we play as well. Most children, if asked what their favorite game is today would respond with some PlayStation or Xbox video game title. Computer games are cool, but they don't physically engage children with each other in the same way that traditional active and participatory games do. They don't get your clothes dirty, and they *certainly* won't make you burst into the kitchen desperate to quench your thirst before running out the door again, exhaling "We're winning by two!"

My mom used to say, "I'll give you something to do!" after hearing me whine about being bored on a weekend morning. Of course, as soon as I heard those words come out of her mouth, I would be side-footing the kickstand of my bike and skidding off to an adventure - anything was better than being at home on a spring, summer, fall or winter's day cleaning windows!

The neighborhood was our extended family. Communities were connected by the footprints of local children hurrying back and forth to each other's houses, coming together to search for adventure and treasure. Neighborhood play breathed life into the community. We used our imagination and creativity to find adventure and fun. And we played.

In this book, I recollect some of the games that we played when I was growing up in New York during the 1970s and 1980s. These are games that engaged us as children. They brought us together as a community for a few hours each day and effectively solved all of our individual problems. They made us run, sweat, get dirty, scream and laugh. They gave purpose to our lives. We were children, and that's what we did. That's what we were supposed to do. We played!

CHAPTER ONE POTATO

COMING TOGETHER

It always seemed to happen naturally, but looking back there was a process that brought the gang together each day. Inspired by the threat of chores if we remained idle for too long in our homes, one friend would start the process by calling over to a buddy's house to get permission. The two friends would then decide who else was needed for conscription. Normally, this sort of carry on would be happening all around the neighborhood at the same time. Multiple small groups of twos or threes would meet up occasionally, moving en-masse for a big event.

Unless we were regrouping to finish something already started, the objective remained unclear until we knew how many players were available. We were flexible though, and what we *did* was secondary to getting together to do it. A small group of two might decide to play h-o-r-s-e until others came along with the potential for a bigger game. A group of three might play base runners or wait until there were three more to play cops and robbers on their bikes or stickball.

So much depended on how much time we had. A free Saturday would allow us the time to organize something big, like the neighborhood Olympics or a proper game of street hockey or kickball. Sometimes, there would be several different games played throughout the day leading up to one big main event.

It didn't really matter what we played as long as we got together and ran around the place, jumping hedges and cutting through alleys to be with our friends. On rainy days, we would scamper around between showers, although there were generally fewer participants on wet days. Our reach was limited and a porch can only accommodate so many at one time.

Where we ended up depended on what game was selected as we gathered the players. For games needing a basketball court, we'd set our mental compass for anyone's house with one or a nearby park if our friend's court wasn't big enough for the size of the game. For street games, like kick-the-can or street hockey, it was generally the street with the least amount of traffic. For field games like Red Rover or Capture the Flag, we would either go to someone's back yard, if it was big enough, or to a neutral, nearby field.

Generally, there were suitable areas for everything, and more often than not certain places became associated with certain games. Over time, you came to know every blade of grass on a particular stretch of lawn. You knew where the dips were, which plants had thorns, and exactly when to accelerate to make it to the safety zone before puttering out. It didn't take long to know the best places to hide in every yard. What bushes were checked first and which had the best escape routes when IT came too near.

We knew our neighborhood inside and out, and there was never a problem finding a suitable venue for any game. Funny, we were rarely *in* any of our friends' houses, but we knew their back yards like the back of our own hand.

MAKING RULES

Regardless of how often we played certain games, the rules always had to be defined before play began each time. This was an important ritual, especially when there was a new boy or girl in the group. Because everyone was familiar with the various versions of the rules, it was more a matter of agreeing on which version would be adhered to. In two-on-two basketball, for example, a standard version was make-it-take-it, meaning if you score a basket, you have control of the ball again.

Not only did rules structure play, but the whole language of rules made the experience familiar and personal. "Make-it-take-it," "no time outs," "safe," "off limits" and "out of bounds" were all phrases that became an integral part of our English vocabulary as children.

The process of making and agreeing on rules could take some time and was generally achieved by vocal consensus. Rules would often be adapted if there were younger children playing so that the older, more athletic players would be handicapped to make it fairer for everyone. The older children liked this, as it challenged them to make it to "home" on one leg or to play with their hands behind their back or tag with their elbows instead of their hands. No challenge was too difficult for the seasoned game player.

PICKING "IT"

Like it or not, many games require that somebody is "IT". Tag, hide-and-seek, monkey in the middle and blind-man's bluff are just a small list of the games that need somebody to be "IT". Often, somebody in the group would volunteer to be "IT", but normally official protocol was followed for the honor. This was the fairest way and also part of the ritual of game playing for children. Everybody was "IT" at one point or another, and some even liked being "IT" because it gave them the power to make someone else "IT".

There are as many ways to select "IT" as there are games to play. If time was precious, we would just draw straws (actually, blades of grass of twigs). The short stick was "IT". More often than not, though, picking "IT" was a poetic song and dance involving rhymes and fists or feet. Everyone would stick one of their feet or fists (thumb-side up generally) into the center of a group and a rhyme was chanted as each foot or fist was touched. Basically, there are two different versions of selecting "IT" in this fashion. Either the first person selected is "IT" or they are freed and the last person remaining is "IT". Again, which version was used depended quite often on how much time we had to play. As each word (or syllable) in the rhyme was said out loud, a foot or fist would be hit (not too hard, but not too softly either!). The foot or hand that was hit as the last word in the rhyme was said would either be "IT" or freed. Sometimes, children used two feet or two fists, thus requiring the elimination of both for selection. Oh yes, there are many rules for selecting who is "IT" and often the rules for selecting "IT" would take as long as the rules of the game itself. Here are some of the rhymes that we used to select "IT".

• • • • • • • • • • •

One potato

Two potato

Three potato

Four

Five potato

Six potato

Seven potato

More

So when "more" was said, the child whose
foot or hand was hit would either be "IT",
"Free" or take one hand or foot out, leaving
the other in to continue the selection process.

• • • • • • • • • • •

Eany, meany, miney, mo

Catch a tiger by his toe

If he hollers, let him go

Eany, meany, miney, mo

• • • • • • • • • •

Engine, engine, number nine

Going down the Hudson Line

If the train falls off the track

Do you get your money back?

At this point, whoever was hit when "back"
was said would say yes or no. If they said
"yes", the rhyme would continue as follows:

y-e-s spells yes, and you can
have your money back.

• • • • • • • • • • •

My mother and your mother

were hanging up clothes

My mother punched your

mother right in the nose

What color was the blood?

(Again, the person who was hit as "blood"

was said would select a color. If they se-

lected red, it would continue as follows)

r-e-d spells red.

• • • • • • • • • • •

The selection of "IT" was as important as the game itself. It was an aesthetic element of coming together to play. Even the physical proximity of the group was tightened when selecting "IT" as everyone had to stand close with feet or fists together. It was as much an element of bonding with your friends as playing the game was.

PICKING TEAMS

Many games required the players to divide into teams. In some neighborhoods, the teams remained the same each time. Other times, different teams formed each day. When there were an even number of skilled players and non-skilled players, we usually split the teams up evenly based on skill so that there would be no unfair advantages.

When picking new teams, the two best players (most people knew who they were) would take turns selecting a player from the gang. It was never nice to be the last one picked, but hey, it happened sometimes. Most children were picked last at one point or another as their skill level evolved over the years. Hey, we just wanted to play. Whether you got picked last or first didn't matter, you were in the game!

Coming together, making rules, selecting "IT" and picking teams set the stage for hours of active fun. In the following chapters, some of the all-time great games will be described so that children today can experience them, and so that the old gang can remember.

CHAPTER TWO POTATO

STREET GAMES

The Street. Our street. Your Street? My Street! Any street could be transformed into a football field, a baseball diamond, a hockey rink, a track and a great place to kick a can. Every part of the street was used. The manhole covers were bases or safe places. The telephone poles were starting and finishing lines, even end zones at times. Streetlights, if you were lucky enough to have them on your street, gave a few extra minutes of play; but also signaled that it was time to head home.

Obviously, we're not talking about major Interstate routes here. Street games were always played on neighborhood streets with good visibility and not much through traffic.

Unfortunately for children today, there are more cars on the roads than there were when I was growing up and safety issues are even more important today. That said, parents know what streets are safe to play on. We used to have a very basic alert signal when a car was heard or seen approaching. "CAR!" we would shout, and play would be suspended until the car passed by. This was somewhat of an inconvenience, but it never bothered us too much and there is something magical about playing on the street, with naturally defined boundaries and long stretches to run.

Here are some street game favorites. Most of them can be played in alternate venues if safe streets aren't available in your neighborhood. That said, they were part of the street and should be played there if possible.

KICK-THE-CAN

What you need: An old coffee can

Ideally played: In the street

HOW TO PLAY:

This is a great game of cat and mouse. Place the can in the center of the street. One person is selected to be "IT". That person starts the game by standing with their foot on the can, facing away from everyone and counting to 30 with their eyes closed while everyone else hides.

Unlike hide-and-go-seek, the hiders don't actually try to stay completely out of sight, just enough so that "IT" can't see them clearly. This is because the hiders have to keep and eye on what's going on. When "IT" sees you, she has to call you out by name. For example, "I see Jody behind the red car." If it *is* Jody behind the red car, then she must go to jail (which is behind the can.) If it *isn't* Jody, then the person doesn't come out from hiding.

The hiders are not allowed to stay in one spot, so when "IT" isn't looking in their direction, they shift around from place to place, being careful that they aren't seen. "IT" can wander as far from the can as she wants to, but must be careful not to stray too far; because when somebody is in jail, the others can free them by running up and kicking the can before they are tagged by "IT".

If "IT" tags them when they're running towards the can, they have to go to jail too. If they manage to kick the can before "IT" tags them, then everyone in jail is freed and "IT" has to count to 30 again with her eyes closed while everyone hides again. The object is for "IT" to capture everyone. When this happens, the first person captured becomes "IT".

Often, those in jail give signals to the remaining people hiding when they have a chance to get to the can before "IT" so they can be freed.

COPS AND ROBBERS

What you need: A bicycle, preferably with homemade handlebars and a playing card playing percussion on the spokes!

Ideally played: In the street

HOW TO PLAY:

A group of six or more are divided into two teams. One team is the 'cops' and the other is the 'robbers'. The 'robbers' get a ten minute head start to hide in the neighborhood. In one version, both the 'cops' and 'robbers' have to stay together in their groups, in another they can split up. The object of the game is basically for the 'cops' to find and pursue the 'robbers' until they find and catch up to them. When playing the version which allows the teams to split up, you'll often find the 'robbers' taking off in different directions when the cops are in hot pursuit. At that point, each individual 'robber', when caught, becomes a 'cop' and helps try to catch the other 'robbers'.

This game is best when the neighborhood has lots of small streets to hide in, but is always exciting, especially if you're a 'robber'. When the 'robbers' are found and caught, the teams switch roles and the 'cops' become the 'robbers'. There are many different versions to this game and normally, children make up their own rules each time. Some have safety zones, some use bags of loot (a bag of pebbles perhaps) that the cops hide and the robbers have to find without getting caught. Others require that the robbers have to be tagged to be caught, but that can be somewhat treacherous when you're barreling down a hill at 25 miles per hour!

STICKBALL

What you need: A broom handle and a rubber ball (preferably a Spalding Pink!)

Ideally played: In the street

HOW TO PLAY:

There are so many different versions of stickball. If you have enough players to have a catcher, this is an awesome street game. Otherwise, it's nice to have a wall behind the batter with a chalk box for the strike zone. Ideally, you will have a pitcher, infielder, outfielder and a batter (but if played in a courtyard with walls, you can play with as few as two players).

In the street, balls were delivered to the batter either as a slow, one-bounce pitch by a pitcher or al fungo (throwing the ball up yourself and hitting it after one bounce). When played in a courtyard with a wall behind the batter, fast pitch normally reigned. Normally, rules specified that a ground ball, not stopped and controlled by a fielder was a single (others discounted ground balls). A fly ball over the pitcher was a single. A fly ball dropped by the outfielder was a double and a fly ball over the outfielder was a triple. A home run was usually determined by a distance marker. If you played 3-on-3, one of the batting team members would act as catcher if played in the street and the other would be the make-believe runner on the bases, advancing bases as determined by the hitting rules. In stickball, bases weren't covered defensively, so there wasn't any tagging out or actual base running. As in baseball, the side was retired after three, but sometimes two outs.

There was also a version of stickball called half-ball, where the pimple ball was actually cut in half for play. The half-ball was held by the pitcher between the index finger and the thumb and delivered with a spin so that it looked like a full ball to the batter. Half balls were easy to hit and thus, one strike was normally considered an out. Stickball, what a game!

STREET HOCKEY

What you need: Street hockey sticks (plastic heads) and a ball or street puck

Ideally played: In the street

HOW TO PLAY:

Street hockey is great fun and is played much like regular ice-hockey, although there are generally fewer players and, well no ice! Goal posts are usually marked by coats or shirts or shoes if it's a roller-hockey game. Street hockey is played by two opposing teams of between four and six children. Each team has a goal keeper, defensive and offensive players. For games with fewer participants, all players generally play both offense and defense.

The object is simply to pass the puck or ball to team members and score a goal by shooting the ball through the goal without the goal keeper stopping it. The team with the most goals at the end of the designated playing time wins. If there are enough players for offense and defensive lines, the offside rule may apply, where an offensive player can't position herself quietly behind the defensive players near the goal waiting for a pass.

If there are only two available players, they can play penalty shoot out, where they alternate places between goal keeper and shooter. After the agreed number of shots on goal, the highest score wins.

ROUND-THE-BLOCK RACES

What you need: Your feet, your bicycle, and sometimes a head start

Ideally played: In the street

HOW TO PLAY:

This game can be played on its own or as an event in a neighborhood Olympics competition. Basically, it is a foot or bicycle race around the block of your neighborhood.

There are also versions for around-the-house races. When different age groups are running together, the younger children can start ahead of the older ones and get a head start. Sometimes, if two runners were competing, they would each go around the house in different directions so they would meet each other half way and be able to gauge if they were ahead or not.

Other variations include race walking, where the children aren't allowed to run, but must walk the entire way (as fast as they can). Judges are required for the walking race so that nobody takes off running when out of site.

NERF FOOTBALL

What you need: A Nerf Football, a light touch and good hands

Ideally played: In the street

HOW TO PLAY:

I was always proud of my Nerf spiral. The trick was not to overthrow it, and to follow through with a smooth and full arm extension. A Nerf Football is a hard spongy ball shaped like a football but smaller. The objective of Nerf Football is to score more touchdowns than the opposing team. Each team has 4 downs or plays to score a touchdown. In Nerf Football, players threw the ball rather than kicking it to change possession. Throwing the Nerf Football was much more effective than kicking it. On the street, we would obviously play two-hand-touch, and certainly if it rained earlier.

PUNCHBALL

What you need: Your fist and a rubber ball (ideally a super pinky!)

Ideally played: In the street

HOW TO PLAY:

Standard baseball rules apply to punch ball for the most part except that there is sometimes no pitcher as the batter bounces the ball to himself. In punch ball, players strike the ball with their closed fist, using their hand instead of a bat. Also, unlike baseball, foul balls are considered strikes. In punch ball, there are two teams. The players determine how many innings will be played and how many outs are allowed per team each inning. Runners can be tagged out and forced out. But, in contrast to baseball, runners in punch ball can also be thrown out if hit with the ball when running to a base. This is a risky play for the defender, because if he misses the runner, the ball can escape and the runner can advance. The object of the game is to score more runs than the other team in the number of innings agreed.

SLAPBALL

What you need: Your palm and a rubber ball
(ideally a super pinky!)

Ideally played: In the street

HOW TO PLAY:

Slap ball is played the same way as Punch ball, except that a pitcher is used who bounce-pitches a ball to the hitter who hits it with his open hand, as opposed to a clenched fist. The hitter must bounce-hit the ball in the infield, so that there are no high fly balls or big popups. In slap ball, runners can be tagged out or forced out, like in baseball. It's more of an infield game for smaller areas, perfect for a narrow street. Home plate was usually a man-hole cover.

FRISBEE FOOTBALL (OR ULTIMATE FRISBEE)

What you need: A Frisbee and a good stop-and-go move

Ideally played: In the street

HOW TO PLAY:

Two teams are picked and end zones and out-of-bounds rules established. Play begins either by the defending team kicking off (throwing the Frisbee to the offensive team) or by the offensive team starting off from several yards in front of their goal line. Either way, the offensive team develops plays, like in regular football, to get the Frisbee into their opponent's end zone. The quarterback can run behind his line, but players cannot run after they catch the Frisbee. The next play starts where the Frisbee was caught.

Depending on how long the street is; rules can be modified as necessary. For example, for a short street, players might determine that there are no first downs and each team has four plays to get a touch down. On fourth down, the offensive team can either go for a touchdown or punt (throw the Frisbee to the other team trying to make them start as close to their end zone as possible.) If the offensive team doesn't get a touchdown on fourth down, the other team starts play at that spot. For larger stretches of road, players might decide to grant first downs after three consecutive catches. Defensive teams can intercept the Frisbee and give their team possession, but again, they cannot run with the Frisbee after catching it.

BATBALL (OR HIT THE BAT)

What you need: A broom handle and a tennis ball

Ideally played: In the street

HOW TO PLAY:

One person is picked to be the batter and the others take places, scattered in the street. The hitter pitches the ball to himself using a toss-and-bounce and the other players field the ball. The fielder who gets to the ball first can run towards the batter until the batter places the bat down on the street in front of him (placed width ways, exposing the full length of the bat to the field).

When the bat goes down on the ground, the fielder must stop running. From the point that he stops at, he must roll the tennis ball toward the bat. If the ball hits the bat, it will jump. If the batter catches the ball when it jumps, or if the fielder misses the bat, the batter is still "up" [at bat]. If the batter isn't able to catch the ball after it hits the bat, then the fielder who threw it becomes the batter. Each successful turn at bat scores one point. The player with the most points at the end of the game wins.

CURB/STOOP/STEPBALL

What you need: A curb, step or stoop and a ball

Ideally played: In the street

HOW TO PLAY:

Before the game, players determine the order of hitting (i.e. who goes first, second and third.) The first hitter stands facing the curb or step and the other players take positions in the field behind her. The hitter throws the ball into the corner of the step or curb so that it bounces into the air behind her.

The fielders try to either catch it or field it if it is a ground ball. If the fielders either catch a fly ball or stop a grounder on first contact, then the hitter gets an out. Each hitter is allowed three outs per round. If the hitter is unsuccessful at getting the ball into play (if the ball overshoots the curb for example) then the hitter receives a strike. Two consecutive strikes is an out. If the hitter is successful at getting the ball passed the fielders then he scores a point.

Sometimes, players have different scoring systems for ground balls and fly balls that soar over everyone's heads. Others use even more complicated scoring systems where each successful ground ball is a base hit, fly balls dropped by fielders are doubles and fly balls over the fielder's head is a triple.

CHAPTER THREE POTATO

COURTYARD GAMES

Some courtyards had kings. There were stories of promise, of sacrifice, of failure - things to live up to - things to prove. The courtyard could be an intimidating place when you first arrived, but it didn't take long for it to become a 3-ring playground. More often than not, several different games were played simultaneously in the courtyard. Groups of children would be in different areas.

Most games involved every aspect of the courtyard's archi-tecture. The walls, corners, fences were all part of the play-ing area. How convenient that they built these buildings so close to our playground, *around* our courtyard. Courtyards offer great protection from any obstruction, and play is seldom interrupted.

The one time that I sprained my elbow, I was rounding third base towards home during a punchball game in the Assumption School courtyard when my feet slipped on the gravel and down I went like a sack of potatoes. But boy did I wallop that ball! I never did find out if my team was awarded a run for that play. I didn't actually cross home plate, but I would have without any doubt!

One courtyard in my neighborhood became an ice skating rink every winter. The neighbors would fill it with water on the night of a big freeze and the next day children were possessed by Dorothy Hammil and Bryan Trottier. Courtyards were cross functional, cross cultural, cross gender, and cross ability. Your first dodge ball game in a courtyard is a right of passage. I think it might have been part of the courtyard initiation as a matter of fact. Courtyard walls serve as an extra player. Ask any boy who throws his ball against the wall.

This chapter explains the rules for some popular courtyard games.

HOPSCOTCH

What you need: Chalk, a marker to throw (a small pebble) and balance

Ideally played: In the courtyard

HOW TO PLAY:

With chalk, draw a series of connected boxes about eighteen inches square starting with a single box for number one. Above and flush with the first box, center two boxes side by side for numbers two and three. Above that, draw another single box for number four. Keep alternating this format until you have a top box for eight and nine. In each box, write the number starting with one in the single box at the bottom. At the very top, above boxes eight and nine, normally a box is provided as "home" which is a safety zone.

After selecting who goes first, that player tosses the marker into the number 1 box (the nearest box). The marker must land completely within the box, without touching a line or bouncing out. If it doesn't land successfully in the desired box, the player loses a turn. If it does land successfully, the player must hop through the entire court, starting at box one (on one foot for single boxes and with two feet in double boxes). When the player gets to the top, or "home" they are safe, but must then continue back down the numbered boxes, remembering to pick up the marker on the way back. If the player does this successfully, they throw the marker at the next number in sequence and complete the board again, stopping to pick up the marker on the way back again. If, while hopping through the court in either direction the player steps on a line, misses a square or loses her balance, her turn is over and the next player goes. Each player starts each turn where they left off on the previous attempt. The player who makes it through each number on the board first wins!

KICKBALL

What you need: A rubber playground ball, and a good kick

Ideally played: In the courtyard

HOW TO PLAY:

This all-time classic is as fun today as it was 30 years ago! Two teams of anywhere from three to six players are picked. The playing field has 4 bases, including home base, just like in baseball. The players determine how many innings will be played and how many outs per inning each team is allowed.

The defensive team sets up, depending on how many are playing, to cover the field. With one pitcher, the other defensive players will cover the infield and outfield as possible. The pitcher rolls the ball to the kicker who kicks it and tries to get to base before they are hit with the ball from a defending player. If the ball is kicked foul, it is considered a strike. If a kicker misses the ball (which is unusual, but it does happen!) it is considered a strike. Three strikes and the kicker is out. If the ball is caught in the air, the kicker is out.

There are three outs per inning. The team with more points at the end of the game wins! This is a really fun game to play at any age.

S-P-U-D

What you need: A rubber playground ball and good aim

Ideally played: In the courtyard

HOW TO PLAY:

S-P-U-D is a great courtyard game that requires at least three players. One player is selected to be "IT". Whoever is selected as "IT" counts aloud to ten. As "IT" counts, the other players scatter away from "IT". For large areas, boundaries or out of bounds should be set so that people can't run too far away.

When "IT" reaches ten, the other players must stop where they are. "IT" then takes four giant steps toward any other player, normally the closest to them, and throws the ball at them. If the ball hits the person, that person gets an "S" for SPUD. If the ball misses the person, then "IT" gets an "S" for SPUD. The person who was being thrown at then is "IT" and the game continues until all players but one is S-P-U-D, either by being hit four times or missing. Some versions allow the person being thrown at to catch the ball, causing "IT" to get a letter (like in dodge ball).

DODGEBALL

What you need: Several rubber playground balls and courage

Ideally played: In the courtyard

HOW TO PLAY:

This great game gets lambasted for being overly aggressive. In fact, it's great fun! Divide into two teams and mark a rectangular playing area with boundaries and a line in the center between the two teams. Each team has to stay on their half of the court. Several (as many as you desire) balls are thrown into the court and the players scramble for them. Each player with a ball tries to hit a player on the other team with it. If the ball hits the other player, they are out. If the ball is caught, then the person who threw it is out. If the ball bounces before it hits a player, it doesn't count. For safety, it is usually a rule that if a player is hit in the face, the player who threw the ball is out. The game continues until there is only one player remaining.

Another version of dodgeball is played in a circle. One team is inside and the other team outside. The players on the outside throw the balls at the team inside the circle. If a player inside the circle is hit, then they join the team on the outside until there is only one player left inside the circle who wins!

CATS GET YOUR CORNER (KITTY CORNER)

What you need: Several rubber playground balls and fast feet

Ideally played: In the courtyard

HOW TO PLAY:

This great game evolved from dodgeball. It is played when one or more (depending on how many are playing the game) players are "IT". All of the "ITs" stand in the center and get a rubber playground ball. The other players each take a spot in one of four designated corners of the court. When "IT" or a referee yells "Cats get a corner", each player on a corner runs to the next corner (all the same way, either clock-wise or counterclockwise, otherwise there will be chaos!)

As the cats are running from corner to corner, the "IT(s)" in the middle try to hit them with the ball(s). If they are hit before they reach the next corner, then the child hit stands by the person who hit them in the middle. When all of the 'cats' are hit, the player in middle with the most 'cats' beside her wins! This is a really fun and active variation of dodgeball!

JUMP ROPE/DOUBLE DUTCH

What you need: A jump rope or two and rhythm

Ideally played: In the courtyard

HOW TO PLAY:

The rules for jump rope are fairly straightforward. Two children hold each end of the jump rope and another, or several children jump in as a song or rhyme is sung, jumping out when it is done. As simplified as this sounds, the complexities of jumping rope are too vast to cover here. There are so many different styles, rhymes, and levels of difficulty. The beauty of the game is that it can be adapted to every level and creatively arranged to suit all players. Some include tasks in their rhymes such as touching the ground, hopping on one leg, etc. An example of a rhyme that requests the jumper to do specific things is:

Teddy Bear, Teddy Bear, **turn around,** (turn around)

Teddy Bear, Teddy Bear, **touch the ground,** (touch the ground)

Teddy Bear, Teddy Bear, **show your shoe,** (show bottom of your shoe)

Teddy Bear, Teddy Bear, that will do! (Jump out)

Teddy Bear, Teddy Bear, **climb the stairs,** (pretend to climb stairs)

Teddy Bear, Teddy Bear, **say your prayers,** (down on knees)

Teddy Bear, Teddy Bear, **turn out the light,** (reach up)

Teddy Bear, Teddy Bear, say good night! (jump out)

Double Dutch is an art form. It is uses two ropes swinging simultaneously in opposite directions and incorporates very athletic maneuvers accomplished to rhyme. There are many national and international Double Dutch competitions and many consider it a sport. Amazing to watch, difficult to do!

HANDBALL

What you need: A handball, a wall and a good back

Ideally played: In the courtyard (or local handball court)

HOW TO PLAY:

Handball can be played by two or four people (singles or doubles). Handball is a serious sport for some, and there are many rules associated with the competitive game. When we were young, though, handball was less complicated. Basically, the server drops the ball and hits it on the bounce to the front wall to start play. Players then alternately hit the ball, trying to make the other miss, with sharp angles, confusing lobs, or fast, low kill shots.

Only the server can score points. When the server loses a rally, he relinquishes service. In every case, the ball must hit the front wall before bouncing and must be hit by the player on the first bounce. Games are played in sets, each set being the best of three games to 21. This is a great game when there are only two children and they want the action of a full-on football game. There is a lot of pace in this game and great challenge.

H-O-R-S-E or P-I-G

What you need: A basketball and hoop and a good imagination

Ideally played: In the courtyard

HOW TO PLAY:

After selecting the order of play, one player starts the game by taking a shot at the basket. Before taking the shot, he must explain the shot. "All net from here", "bank shot from here", "off the backboard, then off my head, then swish". If the player makes the shot that he called then all of the other players have to copy that shot. If they miss the shot, they get a letter (either H for Horse or P for Pig). A player who misses enough shots and spells horse or pig is out of the game.

After every player gets a turn to replicate the shot, the player who made it originally gets to create another shot. If he misses the shot, the next player gets to design a shot and gain control of the game. The winner is the last player on the court.

Of course, as we grew older games of 1-on-1, 2-on-2 or 3-on-3 basketball were very much a part of our play. Half court games could always be found in courtyards.

CHAPTER FOUR

BACKYARD GAMES

"Can I go outside?" "Can I play in the backyard?" "Mom, did you like those purple flowers in the garden?" Sloped yards were good for rolling. Long, flat yards were great for races, Capture the Flag and Red Rover. Mature, landscaped gardens were best for hiding. Yards with trees were best for tag or any game that needed a safe place - trees always seemed to be safe.

Each yard had a calling. Each aged with the children who ran around in it. The landscape seemed to mold itself around our movements over the years. Paths were created between some gardens. They were used as secret passages on some days. Escape hatches on other days. Some yards became basketball courts. Ours had a large, compact dirt court in the shape of a key. It just sort of appeared over time, right underneath our feet. Others stretched into football fields with straight, naturally defined sidelines and ample clearings for end zones.

The yard was a familiar place, with every corner explored over time. It was dug up, rolled down, run through, jumped over, skidded on and slid into. It was a stadium, a gymnasium - an arena. It smelled of dirt, grass, flowers, tree bark and children.

When a game was played in our yard, we had home field advantage. Nobody knew our yard as good as us. There was something nice about having a game played on our turf. Welcome to my stadium. This is the house of Tom. Fare thee well! So many games were played in the backyard.

Here are some of the all-time greats.

RED ROVER

What you need: At least 6 players, good grips and speed

Ideally played: In the yard

HOW TO PLAY:

Two teams are picked, each with equal numbers. The teams line up across the yard from each other. Each team is joined by holding hands, standing side by side with their arms stretched wide. One team begins the game by shouting "Red Rover, Red Rover, Send Tommy Over!" Tommy then takes off across the yard and attempts to break through one pair of the connected hands.

If the runner succeeds in breaking through the line, he goes back to his team (in some versions, he selects one person from the other team to join his team). If he doesn't make it through on the first attempt, he joins the opposing team. Teams alternate calling someone from the other side until one team has all of the players. If there is one remaining player on one team at the end, he can attempt a solo extra point attempt at breaking through. If he makes it, he is the individual champion and the team is the team champion. Either way, nobody loses in this game!

TAG

What you need: A few players and someone with the cooties

Ideally played: In the yard

HOW TO PLAY:

Tag can be played everywhere, but it's a great garden game. In tag, somebody must be picked to be "IT". The objective is for "IT" to tag somebody else. If they manage to catch and tag somebody else, then the person they tag becomes "IT", and play continues until everyone is exhausted. There are many variations of tag which make the game fun when there are a lot of players or if there are players of different abilities (i.e. younger children and older children.)

FREEZE TAG

Freeze tag is played the same way as tag except that when "IT" tags somebody, they are frozen in the place they were tagged. They cannot move from that spot unless another free player is able to crawl between their legs without getting tagged herself. The game is played until every person is frozen. The first person to be frozen is "IT" for the next round.

ELBOW TAG

Elbow tag is the same as tag except that children must use their elbows instead of their hands to tag the others. This is a good rule to use for older children if there are younger children playing.

HOSPITAL (OR STICKY) TAG

Again, the basic rules are the same, except that when you are tagged, you can cover your "wound" with one hand and keep playing. If you are tagged again, you cover your wound with your second hand. The third time you are tagged, you are out.

PARTNER TAG

Partner tag is great fun if there are enough children to play. Players have to select one person to be "IT" and another to be on her own. Basically, everyone else forms groups of two, with their arms linked. When the game begins, "IT" chases after the single runner. She must link with one of the pairs before being tagged. If she manages to link to a grouped pair, the person in that pair who she isn't linked with is set free and "IT" must chase him. When "IT" does tag someone, they change places. What a fun game!

There are many different varieties of tag, many made up on the spot. Later, in the indoor games section, we'll talk about flashlight tag.

DUCK, DUCK, GOOSE

What you need: A circle of children, some ducks and a goose

Ideally played: In the yard

HOW TO PLAY:

All children except one sit in a large circle facing inwards. Each child in the circle should be about two arm lengths away from the child next to them. The player selected to be "IT" walks around the outside of the circle, tapping each player on the head and saying "duck" each time that she touches a players head. At some point, "IT" will call out "goose" instead of duck.

At that point, the person who was tapped to be goose must jump up and chase "IT" around the circle and catch "IT" before she sits in their seat. If the goose catches "IT" before she gets around to the seat, then "IT" continues to be "IT". Otherwise, the goose is "IT". There's nothing quite like running around in circles at breakneck speed!

CAPTURE THE FLAG

What you need: Enough players and a flag (go on, use your imagination!)

Ideally played: In the yard

HOW TO PLAY:

Again, two teams are needed for this one. Each team has a side of the yard and a flag. Each team also decides where the jail will be on their side. The objective of the game is to capture the other team's flag and secure it on your side without getting tagged. Each team is usually allowed to have no more than two players guarding their flag. Players can only be tagged when on their opponent's side of the field. If a player is tagged, they must go to jail. They can be freed from jail if someone on their team grabs their hand and runs with them to their own side of the field without getting tagged. If they are tagged, then both must go to jail. No team can have guards at their jail. When one team manages to grab their opponent's flag and carry it over to their side, they win. This is another great game of cat and mouse.

In another version, a football is used as the flag and a player can throw the ball back to his side when he grabs it, but the ball must be caught in order for it to count.

STEAL THE BACON

What you need: Just a piece of bacon (I'm kidding!). A glove or ball will do.

Ideally played: In the yard

HOW TO PLAY:

Once again, two teams are selected for this game. If there is an extra person, they can be the referee. The bacon is placed in the middle of the field, equidistant between the two teams. Each team member is assigned a number from one to ten. When the referee shouts out a number, that number from each team comes forward on their side. No other players from either team can go over their line into the field of play.

When the referee shouts "Go", both players approach the bacon in the middle. The object of the game is to grab the bacon from the ground and run back to your side without getting tagged by the other player. If this is done, your team gets a point. If you get tagged, the other team gets a point.

There are many different strategies. Some players race in trying to beat the other player to the bacon. Other times it becomes a chess game, waiting to see who snatches it first. A player can only be tagged after she grabs the bacon.

The first team to score ten points wins.

In other versions of Steal the Bacon, several numbers are called in at once, creating teams. The strategy really heats up in this version. The bacon can be passed or thrown until it gets over to your side. Again, only the person with the bacon can be tagged.

BASE RUNNERS

What you need: At least 3 players, a ball, baseball mitts (optional), and good timing

Ideally played: In the yard

HOW TO PLAY:

This is a great game when there are only three players available. After picking who is "IT", the other two players put on the gloves and stand at the two bases. The bases are set up across from each other, with a good bit of room between them. Basically, this is a game of base running.

Almost like monkey in the middle, except that rather than trying to catch the ball that the basemen are throwing, the runner tries to avoid it. The runner times running from base to base so as not to get tagged out at the plate. If he gets tagged, then he changes places with the person who tagged him.

It is possible to play this game with more than three people. If there are more than three, then select two players to be "IT" at the beginning and alternate throwers as tags are made. A fantastic game that requires agility, speed, and a good throwing arm. Definitely a yard game if you have children who would be apt to slide into the plate!

KILL THE CARRIER

What you need: Children with high testos-
terone levels

Ideally played: In the yard

HOW TO PLAY:

A game cannot be simpler. A ball is thrown high into the air above a group of players. Whoever catches it tries to avoid the rest of the mob as they attempt to tackle him. There are no real objectives for the carrier aside from keeping hold of the ball for as long as possible. Obviously, there were some rules, like no hitting in the face; no tackling from behind, no clothes lining (sticking your arm out when someone is running by you).

It was just a game, like King of the Hill, where the only point was to chase down a boy with a ball in his hands and try to take it from him. Great fun though.

JAIL BREAK

What you need: Just the gang

Ideally played: In the yard

HOW TO PLAY:

Jail break is a cross between hide and seek and tag in which the player selected to be "IT" tries to find the others and tag them. In jail break, when "IT" tags someone hiding, the person is sent to jail. Jail and safe places are always selected before the game begins. "IT" then tries to find and tag more players until the jail is full. Of course, the free players can sneak over to the jail and step in it, which causes a jailbreak, freeing everyone inside! A wonderful game of hiding, chasing, tagging and freeing!

SARDINES

What you need: Good hiding places and giggling children

Ideally played: In the yard

HOW TO PLAY:

"Shhhh! Stop laughing! He'll hear us!" Sardines is a classic version of hide-and-Seek. In Sardines, one person hides and all the others seek her without letting anyone know when she is found. Confusing? Well, that's because the object of the game is to find the hider and sneak in to hide with her. Eventually, all players except one has found the hiding place. The last person to find the "sardines" packed together under the porch giggling is "IT". This game is all about fun.

THE PRETZEL OR HUMAN KNOT

What you need: A group of limber limbs

Ideally played: In the yard

HOW TO PLAY:

Players face each other in a tight circle. They all extend their hands out to hold another hand until every hand in the circle is held by another. The object is to figure out how to untangle yourselves without letting go of anyone's hand. Like twister in reverse!

WHIFFLE BALL

What you need: A Whiffle bat, a Whiffle ball and good air current

Ideally played: In the yard

HOW TO PLAY:

Nothing curves like a Whiffle ball! Whiffle ball is the short field version of baseball. A Whiffle ball is a white, hollow plastic ball with vents for air current. Whiffle balls can take unpredictable turns and have great motion to them.

Players form two teams. One team hits and the other team fields. The pitcher sends in curves, sliders, and knuckle balls and the batter tries to connect with one. Normal base running could apply or imaginary base runners could be used if there aren't enough players. Each hitter is out if he strikes three times (four fouls in a row is a strike), or if his hit is caught in the air, or if he is thrown out or tagged out. There are three outs for each team every inning.

The team with the most runs at the end of play wins.

SNAKES IN THE GRASS

What you need: Slithering children and quick feet

Ideally played: In the yard

HOW TO PLAY:

This is a fun game. Players pick who's "IT" and determine the out-of-bounds areas. The player selected to be "IT" lays on the ground in the middle of the playing area and the others wander around her until the referee or one of the players shouts "THERE'S A SNAKE IN THE GRASS!".

At that point, the snake tries to tag the players by moving on her belly and extending her arms. When she tags someone, they become a snake as well, making it harder for the others to avoid getting tagged.

The last person tagged is the winner.

Usually, the first player tagged is "IT" for the next round.

THE BIG BAD WOLF

What you need: A wolf and a few Little Red Riding Hoods

Ideally played: In the yard

HOW TO PLAY:

Players select one person to be the wolf. The other players line up at a designated starting line as the wolf stands facing away from them on the other side of the yard. The players ask the wolf "What time is it Mr. Wolf?" The wolf responds with a time. If the wolf says "It's four o'clock my dears." then the players take four steps toward the wolf. Whatever time the wolf says, the players continue to take that many steps toward him.

At some point in the game, when the players ask the world what time it is, he responds, "It's DINNER TIME!" At that point, the children turn and run back to the starting line before the wolf tags them. If the wolf tags a player before she makes it back to the starting line, then she is "IT" for the next round. Some players keep playing, making each tagged player another wolf. In that version the last player caught by the wolves is the winner.

This game can be played in a swimming pool too.

OBSTACLE COURSE

What you need: A good imagination and versatility

Ideally played: In the yard

HOW TO PLAY:

Obstacle courses are great fun when players get creative. They can also be very challenging and adapted to any skill level. Players work together to create the number and type of obstacles. For example, stage one might include crawling on your stomach from one point to another. Stage two might involve somersaulting five consecutive times. Stage three might involve walking backwards for a certain distance. Stage four might be a sprint back to the finish line.

The only restriction in this game is the players' imagination. Older, more athletic players can adapt the course so that it challenges them, like running around the block instead of around the house. But I've never seen anyone; old, young, fast or slow manage to be spun around ten times and run for twenty yards without finding it challenging!

Some players split up into teams and have relay obstacles. Others conduct heats of two or three players, with the winner of each heat advancing to the next round. Any way you slice it, it's great fun!

MINE FIELD

What you need: A good sense of direction

Ideally played: In the yard

HOW TO PLAY:

Two teams are selected and the field of play is agreed. One team acts as mines, spread out randomly in the field of play. The other team has to get their players across the field to the other end without bumping into any of the mines. Oh, did I not mention that the players are blindfolded! Each team selects a guide to help their team cross safely by shouting directions to her teammates. "Stop! Move to your left!"

Each player that navigates through the course without hitting a mine scores a point for their team. When all players from one team are safely across the field or blown up by the mines;

it is their turn to be mines and the other team goes. The team that has the most points at the end of play wins.

THE FLYING DUTCHMAN

What you need: Good rounding speed

Ideally played: In the yard

HOW TO PLAY:

There is nothing as exhilarating as running fast around a circle. In The Flying Dutchmen, players form a large circle and hold hands with the player on either side of them. One player is selected to be "IT".

"IT" walks around the outside of the circle and taps one set of joined hands. When he does, the two players whose hands were tapped take off, like, well like Flying Dutchmen, in opposite directions around the outside of the circle.

Meanwhile, "IT" has already stepped in to one of their spots, so there's only one spot left, and the flying Dutchman who makes it back first gets it. The other is "IT"! Like Duck, Duck, Goose, but runners go in opposite directions, causing even more havoc.

UNCLE SAM or POM POM

What you need: Plenty of players and colors

Ideally played: In the yard

HOW TO PLAY:

There are several versions of this game, but we grew up with Uncle Sam. One player is picked to be "IT". "IT" stands in the middle of a playing field with the other players at one end in a safe zone.

The object is to run across the playing field to the other safe zone without getting tagged. To start, players in the safe zone ask: "Uncle Sam, may we cross your river dam?" "IT" responds selectively using some criteria. For example, if color was used as the criteria, then "IT" would respond, "Yes you may, if you're wearing blue today."

At that point, every player wearing blue would have to run over to the other side without getting tagged. If they were tagged, they would help "IT" in the middle. The first person tagged would be "IT" for the next game.

The last player tagged is the winner.

PENALTY SHOOTOUT

What you need: A soccer ball and a goal

Ideally played: In the yard

HOW TO PLAY:

This is a great game when there are only two players around. Basically, it's just like a regular soccer penalty shootout. The players determine the distance from the goal and the size of the goal. Goal posts can be shirts, jackets, bushes, trees, or anything else available to the players if a proper soccer net isn't available in the backyard.

Usually, players pretend it's the end of a very close game between two great teams and there is great excitement to see who will win the game by taking penalties. Penalty Shoot Out provides wonderful opportunities to dive for a ball! Don't wear your Sunday best for this game.

BLIND MAN'S BLUFF

What you need: A blindfold and caution

Ideally played: In the yard

HOW TO PLAY:

Blind-man's bluff is great fun for all ages. One player is selected to be "IT" and a playing area is marked. "IT" is blindfolded and put in the center of the playing area. The object is for the blindfolded "IT" to tag somebody without seeing them. The other players can move around freely within the designated field of play.

Sometimes, a player might sneak up close to "IT" to confuse her by saying something and then moving away before she tags them. But be careful, sometimes, "IT" suspects this and turns quickly every now and then for a tag. When "IT" tags someone, they are "IT" and a new game is started. Otherwise, some players keep blindfolding everyone who is tagged and the last person tagged is the winner.

MONKEY IN THE MIDDLE

What you need: At least three players, a ball, and springs in your shoes

Ideally played: In the yard

HOW TO PLAY:

Monkey-in-the-middle is a game of keep away. One person is chosen to be the monkey ("IT") and stands in the middle of the other players while they throw a ball or other object around. The monkey in the middle tries to intercept a pass and catch the ball.

The monkey isn't allowed to touch the other players or step into the safe zones where they are playing. It doesn't take long for a pass to fall short or to be thrown too low, allowing the monkey to intercept it. The player who throws the ball that the monkey intercepts is declared "IT" and a new game begins. This is a great game to practice your jumping!

CABOOSE OR LOOSE CABOOSE

What you need: At least seven players with good zig-zagging ability

Ideally played: In the yard

HOW TO PLAY

One player is selected to be "IT". The other players form trains of three players, each holding on to the hips of the person in front of them. The first person in each train set is the engine. The object is for "IT" to attach on to the end of one of the trains as they snake around the playing area.

If "IT" is able to attach himself onto one of the trains, the engine (lead player) of that train becomes the loose caboose ("IT") and a new game is started. The trains can dodge, twist and turn all they want to prevent "IT" from attaching on, but they must always stay connected with both hands on the hips of the player in front of them.

LEAP FROG

What you need: A good back and a high hop

Ideally played: In the yard

HOW TO PLAY:

Leap frog is a classic game that involves players jumping over each other in sequence. One person jumps over the other players by putting his hands on their back and springing over like a frog as they are crouched down with their hands on the ground. After jumping the last player, the jumper then takes a crouched position in the front of the line. The player at the back of the line starts jumping to the front as soon as someone jumps over them. This way, there is a continuous movement of jumpers that moves forward each time.

Some players attempt to keep the line moving until they make it around the yard completely without a mistake. Others turn it into a race with two different teams competing over a specified distance. Either way, you'll sleep well after playing this one for a while!

AT THE RACES

What you need: Speed, strength and stamina

Ideally played: In the yard

HOW TO PLAY:

The only thing limiting the amount of races that can be run in the backyard is a player's imagination. Races can be adapted for any size of yard or age of player. Here are a few races that I remember fondly:

Wheelbarrow Races

Players select a start and finish line and form groups of two. One person in each team is the wheelbarrow and the other moves the wheelbarrow across the yard to the finish line. The wheelbarrow has his hands on the ground as his teammate holds his feet in the air. To move, the wheelbarrow must move his hands as fast as possible to get across to the finish line.

Egg and Spoon Races

Each player has a spoon and an egg. Players place the egg on the spoon and hold it in front of them as they run to the finish line. The trick is keeping the egg in the spoon as you move forward. Some feel it's better to go slower and maintain control, others try to go fast. If your egg falls, you have to start at the beginning again. Now, unless you want to go through a lot of eggs, consider using small potatoes or hard-boiled eggs. For high risk though, there is no substitute for a raw egg.

Baby-Step Races

Baby-step races are great for smaller yards or when there is a range of abilities participating. The objective, like in most races, is to try to get to the finish line first. But in this race, players have to move by placing the heel of one foot in front of the toes of the other foot.

Island Races

In island races, each player has two pieces of cardboard or something similar that they can stand on. The object is to move forward by placing one piece of board down, stepping on it and then placing the next one down in front until you get to the finish line. Players must only move forward if they are stepping onto a piece of their island. If a player steps off of their island at any time during the race, they have to start at the beginning again.

Potato Sack Races

What a classic! Players step into a sack of some sort, burlap or some other strong material preferably, and hop down the course to the finish line. This is harder than it looks!

Three-Legged Races

Another classic! Players group in teams of two. Each team is joined by tying the left leg of one teammate with the right leg of the other. Working together, they move as fast as they can to get to the finish line before the other teams. This is great fun!

CHAPTER
FIVE
POTATO

PORCH GAMES

Ours was a patio more than a porch, over the garage slightly in front of the house, on the left as you approached the front door. The eaves of the front roof came out a good distance so we could sit out even when it rained.

Some porches have screen windows all around and an aluminum door. My neighbors had a lovely screened porch in their back garden. It had electricity and everything in it. But porches should be at the front of the house really. Some porches wrap around houses. Others are just steps at the front door, but you could spend hours there happily.

A porch is a place to look out from - a place to sit on summer nights and hear crickets - a place to smell the rain hitting the ground in front of you. A porch is a place to wait for the game to begin or a place to talk about it when it's over. A porch is a great hiding place, jail and safe zone. A porch is somewhere to cool off. For children, a porch is another place to play.

JACKS

What you need: A set of Jacks, fast reflexes and good coordination

Ideally played: On the porch

HOW TO PLAY:

Players decide the order of play and then pour the jacks out onto the floor. To do this, seasoned Jacks players will flip. Flipping is taking all ten jacks and placing them in both hands, flipping them into the air and catching them with the backs of your hands. Then, the player flips them again while turning their hands palm-side up again. The player who catches the highest amount of Jacks in this fashion begins the game.

The objective of the game is to make your way through from onesies (picking up one jack) to tensies (picking up all ten jacks) and then back in reverse order to onesies. Each player in turn throws the ball up and picks up the correct number of jacks.

On the first turn, players start with onesies; so the player tosses the bouncing ball in the air, and picks up one jack in time to catch the ball after it bounces once, still holding the jack in her hand, and using only one hand. If they complete onesies, then they do the same for twosies, picking up two jacks this time, and so on up to tensies. Each player continues her turn until she either misses picking up the right amount of jacks, catching the ball on one bounce, or dropping a jack when catching the ball. Obviously, this game gets harder as you move closer to ten.

For each turn, the player must complete the round until all jacks are picked up. For example, when trying onsies, the player throws the ball up, picks up one jack, catches the ball. Then she has to do it again until all ten jacks are picked up.

For twosies, the player would have to successful pick two jacks up five different times. For fivesies, the player would have to pick up 5 jacks twice.

Obviously, there are some numbers that will leave an odd number. For sixies, the player would pick up six jacks the first time and then there would be four jacks left. The odd jacks left are called the" cart". In rounds where "carts" exist (threesies, foursies, sixies, sevensies, eightsies, and ninesies), a player can pick up the odd "cart" before the even number, but if they do, they need to call out "CART" before picking the odd number of jacks up.

The object of the game is to be the first player to successfully complete all rounds to tensies and back down to onesies.

For more advanced Jacks players, there are special rounds called fancies. Fancies are special rules that might include picking up the Jacks in a certain way or allowing flipping to be done until a certain round level, like "flip to fivesies".

Playing Jacks is a wonderful way to spend time on your porch on a warm, rainy afternoon.

ROCK, PAPER, SCISSORS

What you need: A poker face and some luck

Ideally played: On the porch

HOW TO PLAY:

Rock-paper-scissors is sometimes used to pick who goes first, but is at times played as a game by itself. Two players flash hand signals at the same time. There are three different symbols that can be flashed; a rock, which is shown by a closed fist; paper, which is shown by an open hand; and scissors, which is demonstrated by the index and middle fingers separated.

The rules are quite simple. Scissors cuts paper, so if one player shows the sign for paper and the other player chooses scissors, then the latter player showing scissors wins the round. Paper covers rock, so the player showing the paper symbol beats the player using rock. Rock crushes scissors, so the player showing rock beats the player showing scissors. The players determine how many rounds will be played, and the winner is determined by who wins the most rounds.

The presentation of the hand symbol is rather dramatic. Players face each other with their fists moving up and down in front of them as they chant "Rock, paper, scissors". As "scissors" is said, both players reveal their symbol in front of them.

FLINCH

What you need: A soft ball and good reflexes

Ideally played: On the porch

HOW TO PLAY:

Players sit or stand on the porch with their arms folded in front of them. Any player can start the game by either throwing to ball to another person or faking a throw to them. If the player flinches, or unfolds their arms thinking that the ball is coming to them, then they are out.

Likewise, if the ball is actually thrown to them and they drop it, they are out. The last person in the game is the winner. If there are only a few players, and you want the game to last longer, you can give a player a letter when they drop the ball or flinch. When a player misses enough to spell F-L-I-N-C-H, they are out.

This is a great ball game to play in a small space and is great for developing your reflexes.

HOT POTATO

What you need: A hot potato or other small object to pass around

Ideally played: On the porch

HOW TO PLAY:

Players sit or stand around and pass an object quickly around to each other. When the signal is given, whoever has the "hot potato" in their hands is out. The signal might be the stopping of music like in musical chairs, or it may be a whistle or other signal given randomly by someone not involved in the passing.

Because nobody wants to be caught holding the "hot potato", it doesn't stay in anyone's hands for too long. As a result, this is a very fast moving game.

I SPY

What you need: A keen eye and good observation

Ideally played: On the porch

HOW TO PLAY:

What a fantastic way to whittle away some time on a porch. This simple game is real fun and can be played by people of any age, making it great for families to play together. One player starts the game by saying: "I spy with my little eye, something red."

The other players then attempt to guess what object the first player is thinking of. Any descriptive word can be used, it doesn't have to be a color. "I spy with my little eye, something furry, tiny, hot, shiny, or blue." The person who guesses correctly gets to be the next spy.

ARM WRESTLING

What you need: Good biceps, deltoids and forearm muscles

Ideally played: On the porch

HOW TO PLAY:

Ah, the ultimate test for comparing strength, and the biggest don't always win. Two players sit facing each other and lock hands, palm to palm with their elbows on a table. When the signal is given, the players attempt to force the other players arm down, touching the back of his hand on the table.

When playing in groups, heats are often organized by picking names for match ups in the first round. Winners in each round go through to the next round. This continues until the final match.

The winner is the player who wins the final contest. If only two people are playing, they will often have a best two out of three competition.

GILLIGAN'S ISLAND

What you need: Enough square pieces of paper for each player to stand on

Ideally played: On the porch

HOW TO PLAY:

Not unlike musical chairs, this fun game is played by scattering islands of paper around the porch so that there is one for everyone to stand on EXCEPT one person. The paper islands should be spaced a good distance from each other, but randomly.

The game begins with the players moving around the porch in a circle, not stopping until the signal is given to get on an island. When the signal is given (either by music stopping or a spectator shouting, "ISLAND") the players must stand on one of the paper islands. Because there is one less island than players, one player will not have an island to stand on, and is out of the game.

For the next round, one more island is taken away, so that there is always one less island than player. This continues until there are only two players and one island left. There's not enough room on this island for the both of us! This is a very fun game to play on the porch some rainy day.

BUBBLE PLAY

What you need: A bottle of good old-fashioned bubbles with a wand

Ideally played: On the porch

HOW TO PLAY:

While it's fun just to sit around and blow bubbles, there are some games to play with bubbles as well. One such game is "bubble building" where players try to stack bubbles on top of each other. Players start by blowing their bubbles and catching one on their wand. Then, with one caught, they attempt to attach another to it. Then another, until the player with the most bubbles connected wins.

Bubble Relay

Bubble relays are great fun for small places. Players divide into teams of two. A player on each team blows bubbles to their teammate. The teammate catches a bubble with their wand and carries it to the end of the porch and back, transferring the bubble carefully to their partner's wand. The partner then has to walk the bubble to the end of the porch and back....all without the bubble popping! The first team to accomplish this wins. If a bubble pops at any time, the team has to start again from the beginning.

PATTY CAKE

What you need: A little rhythm and good coordination

Ideally played: On the porch

HOW TO PLAY:

I dare any boy to say that this is too easy. Patty Cake is a fun, rhythmical game played by chanting a rhyme while clapping hands together with a partner. Two players face each other and begin a series of progressively harder combinations of clapping their hands together, palm to palm while chanting a rhyme such as:

Patty cake

Patty cake

Baker's man

Bake me a cake

As fast as you can

Roll it

and

Pat it

and mark it with B

And put it in the oven for baby and me.

Players clap each other's hands in specific sequences depending on the rhyme used for the game. Two-hand claps, one-hand claps and complex cross-over claps are all part of the routine. This is very interesting to watch, and extremely fun to play.

CHAPTER
SIX
POTATO

SIDEWALK GAMES

Sidewalks or footpaths are avenues to and from places. Some sidewalks are too busy with pedestrians to play on. Other sidewalks are too close to busy roads. But some sidewalks offer a perfect place to spend some time playing a game. At times, sidewalks are used because the grass is too wet to play in.

Other times, children play a game on the sidewalk when they're waiting for their mother to come out of the house or shop. Children from city neighborhoods who didn't have big yards used sidewalks more regularly. Whatever the occasion, sidewalks provide a straight, solid and level field of play that compliments many games.

When walking along a footpath on the way to a game in a field or friend's house, the path itself provided countless possibilities for play. We were told: "Step on a crack and break your mother's back." We didn't really think that our mother's backs would break if we did, but it was enough for us to try avoiding cracks for the rest of the day. Depending on the sidewalk, it was a good challenge to avoid the cracks, especially on old, in-need-of-repair footpaths. And we loved a challenge! Often, the curbs of sidewalks became balancing beams, and we were always one good routine away from taking Gold at the Olympics.

Rumor has it that Carl Lewis started his long jump career by attempting to jump over every other cement square on the sidewalk. Well, that's not true, but we did!

MARBLES

What you need: Some shooters, crystals, chalk and good aim

Ideally played: On the sidewalk

HOW TO PLAY:

Marbles can be played in the dirt or on the sidewalk. Often, there were dirt patches next to sidewalks, but if not then the sidewalk provided a challenging and unpredictable surface to play on. Many different versions of marbles have evolved over the years, and each player has his own preference and style. The most common version, perhaps, is played by drawing one large outer chalk circle with a small bulls-eye circle in the middle.

Players decide how many marbles are initially put in the large circle by each person. These marbles are scattered around inside the large circle. The first player shoots one of his "shoot-ers" at another player's marble in the circle, trying to knock it out of the ring.

The most common shooting method used is pushing the marble out of a curled index fin-ger with your thumb, in the same manner that you would flip a coin into the air. Aim is more important than speed, although you need suf-ficient trajectory to get the marble you hit out of the circle. If you knock a marble out and your marble stays in the circle, then you get to shoot again from the spot where your marble stops. Each marble that a player hits out of the circle is kept by him. If you miss, then the next player shoots. If a player's most valuable mar-ble (and every player has at least one beauty), is hit then he has the option of placing it in the bulls-eye.

The player who hits it has to stand up, stretch his arm out over the circle and attempt to drop one of his marbles on top of the prized marble sitting in the bulls-eye. If the player hits it, then it is his, fair and square. If he misses, then the original owner is spared losing his treasured glass orb. The player who has the most marbles at the end of the game wins.

Be careful though, because this game can be addictive!

RED LIGHT, GREEN LIGHT

What you need: A quick step and a watch-ful eye

Ideally played: On the sidewalk

HOW TO PLAY:

One player is selected to be "the traffic light" and stands in the center of the sidewalk, fac-ing away from the others. The other players line up about twenty or twenty-five feet behind her. When "the traffic light" says "green light", the players can move forward as much as they want. Sounds easy, right?

Well, the difficulty arises when "the traffic light" suddenly shouts "red light". When "red light" is called, "the traffic light" looks around quickly and if she catches anyone moving towards her, they are out of the game. The first player who is able to tag "the traffic light" without being caught moving at a "red light" is the winner.

Some of my earliest childhood memories involve this game. It's an all-time classic.

MOTHER MAY I?

What you need: Giant steps and good manners

Ideally played: On the sidewalk

HOW TO PLAY:

This game is a relation of red light, green light. Players select one person to be "mother" and he stands at one end of the sidewalk, facing away from the other players. The other players stand about 20 feet behind him. "Mother" starts the game by instructing one of the players how many steps to take. For example, "mother" might say, "Tommy, you may take one giant step forward." Tommy must reply "Mother may I?" before taking the steps requested. If he forgets to ask, then he goes back to the starting line. If "mother" replies, "Yes, you may." then Tommy may take one giant step forward.

Now, there are a variety of steps that "mother" can ask the players to take. There are giant steps forward, giant steps backward, baby steps forward, baby steps backward, normal steps forward, normal steps backward, hops forward, hops backward, ballerina twirls forward, ballerina twirls backward, frog jumps forward, frog jumps backward, and any other steps that come to the imagination of "mother".

The first player who reaches "mother" and taps her is the winner. This is a great game for children of all ages!

SIDEWALK ART

What you need: Sidewalk chalk and a great imagination

Ideally played: On the sidewalk

HOW TO PLAY:

Sidewalk art can be played many different ways, but basically it's about having fun creating colorful works of art on the sidewalk. Sometimes, games are devised using sidewalk art. For example, one player might draw a shape in the designated frame and each consecutive player adds another shape or line until a picture appears. Each player is allowed one mark per turn.

Another sidewalk art game is called exhibition. A theme is selected and each player draws something relating to that theme. Each player then puts a score on each completed work, the higher number being the best. Players cannot score their own piece. The player with the most points is the winner of the exhibition.

Often, standard drawing games are played on the sidewalk using chalk. Games like tic-tac-toe, hangman, and boxes can all be played with chalk on the sidewalk.

The sidewalk is a great place to exhibit your talents or just to make the world a more colorful place to live.

HULA HOOP

What you need: A hula hoop and gyrating hips

Ideally played: On the sidewalk

HOW TO PLAY:

I swear that I was able to do this when I was young. Things happen to us as we get older, and one thing that definitely happens is that we lose our ability to hula hoop over time. The hula hoop is a wonderful invention.

Players hold the hula hoop at waist level, with one side of it pressed against their waist. Then, with a twist, they start the hoop in motion and begin to swivel their hips to keep the hula hoop rotating around and around. Good players can make the hula hoop rise and lower on their torso. Excellent players can have several hoops going simultaneously.

Games are played to see who can keep it going the longest or who can use the most hoops at once.

There are also rolling games with the hula hoop. Sometimes, players just roll it back and forth to each other. Other times, they have distance competitions to see who can roll it the farthest. Another variation involves placing a target on the sidewalk to see who can get the hula hoop to land near it or on it. Like horseshoes, if the hula hoop lands within one hula hoop from the target, the player gets one point. If the hula hoop lands touching the target, the player gets three points. If the hula hoop lands around the target (with the target inside the hula hoop), the player gets five points.

The winner is either the player who scores the most points after a pre-determined number of rounds or the first to reach a pre-determined score (first to get 21).

CHAPTER SEVEN POTATO

INDOOR GAMES

The call, "It's time to come inside!" was usually met with disappointed sighs; but coming inside isn't necessarily a bad thing – because indoors can be a great place to play too! There's something nice about being inside on a rainy day. Playing indoors opens your eyes to a whole new world under the roof. Closets become secret chambers, beds are ships at sea, and the living room magically transforms into a playing field. Indoors is full of mystery and adventure. When my brother and I were very young, the line between our imagination and thirst for adventure blurred one day, and we soon found ourselves actually tunneling a hole from our bedroom closet into the adjacent closet in our parent's room. We were convinced that there was treasure behind the walls. We were wrong, but there is no end to the fun that can be found when you play indoors.

Indoor play is a nice break from the great outdoors. There is an intimacy that doesn't exist outside. Whether friends stop over to your house, or you go over to theirs, indoors takes on a whole new purpose when play is involved. You see things differently somehow. Often, indoor play involves a party of some kind, which only adds to the brilliance of the venue. It becomes a children's place rather than your parent's house. And children's places are for one thing and one thing only. Play!

HIDE AND SEEK

What you need: Good hiding places and a super seeker

Ideally played: Indoors

HOW TO PLAY:

The classic indoor game! Players select one person to be "IT". He counts to 100 (less if younger children are playing or if there are only a few hiders) while the other players hide in the house. When "IT" is finished counting, he shouts "Ready or not, here I come!", and searches for the players hiding. Each player that he finds has to go to the room (or jail) where "IT" started counting. "IT" continues to seek out the remaining hiders until they are all captured.

Another variation of hide and seek has a safe base. In this version, the hiders come out of hiding as "IT" looks for them and try to make it to the safe base without getting caught. If they are tagged trying to get to the safe place, then they are "IT" for the next game. If all players make it to the safe base, then "IT" has to be the seeker again. If he fails to capture any player again, then he selects someone to be "IT" for the next round. There is a lot of tip-toeing around the house in this version.

HOT AND COLD

What you need: An object to hide and fluctuating temperatures

Ideally played: Indoors

HOW TO PLAY:

One person is selected to be "IT". She has to leave the room while the rest of the players hide an object in the room. When they call "IT" back into the room, she has to find the object that they hid. The players help by dramatically feeling hotter the closer "IT" gets to the object. Likewise, they express how cold they feel when "IT" moves further away from the object. "I'm feeling a little warmer now.", "Oh yea, it's definitely getting very warm in here now!", "Brrrr, it's cold all of a sudden!"

When the player finds the object, she gets to pick the next person to be "IT".

SIMON SAYS

What you need: A Simon and players who listen carefully to him

Ideally played: Indoors

HOW TO PLAY:

One person is selected to be Simon. Simon stands facing everyone and tells the group to perform a variety of movements or activities. Players should only copy Simon if he starts by saying "Simon says..." If Simon simply instructs that an action be performed without saying "Simon says..." the players shouldn't do it. For example: "Simon says touch your toes." On this command, players should touch their toes.

However, if Simon simply directs, "Touch your knees!" any player who does it is out of the game. This gets tricky when a string of commands is heard in quick order. Players who don't do what Simon says when he starts with "Simon says..." are also out of the game. The winner is the last person remaining in the group. My favorite one is throwing in a "Hop!" after a series of progressively fast "Simon says..." commands. It's amazing how many players will hop, knowing that they shouldn't.

SCAVANGER HUNT

What you need: A long list of things to find and people to find them

Ideally played: Indoors

HOW TO PLAY:

Divide the group into teams of equal numbers. Each team is presented with a list of items to find and collect from within the house. The first team to return with all of the items on the list is the winner. The more creative the list of things to find is the more fun the game will be.

Think outside of the box for this one. Ask teams to find a smelly sock, something smaller than your fingernail, something furry, something gross. To make it educational, use things appropriate for each age group.

For younger players, use colors, numbers and letters on the list. For older players, challenge them with advanced vocabulary. Ask older players to find something corrugated or translucent. Have a dictionary handy for them to refer to. This game can also be played in the back yard and even all over town using cars for the older gang.

FLASHLIGHT TAG

What you need: Flashlights and dark rooms

Ideally played: Indoors

HOW TO PLAY:

One player is selected to be "IT" and the other scatter around the house while he counts to twenty. The object is for "IT" to catch each player by shining his flashlight on them. Players determine where safe is before the game begins. If a player is caught in "IT's" beam before she gets to the safe zone, then she is "IT" and must tag another player with her beam of light. This is a fun game for a sleepover.

MUSICAL CHAIRS

What you need: Enough chairs arranged in a circle for all but one player

Ideally played: Indoors

HOW TO PLAY:

Enough chairs for all players except one are arranged in a circle in the middle of the room, seats facing outwards. Players stand outside of the circle of chairs and start walking in a circle around the chairs as the music plays. When the music stops, players rush to take a seat.

The player who is left without a chair to sit on is out of the game. Another chair is taken away for each round so that there is always one less chair than there are players. The game con-tinues until there are only two players and one chair left. The winner of the game is the person who sits down in the last remaining chair. This is a great party game for younger children.

STATUES

What you need: The ability to remain very still at a moment's notice

Ideally played: Indoors

HOW TO PLAY:

All players stand and dance in place while music is being played. When the music stops, the players must become statues, freezing in place without moving a limb. The leader looks around at the group to see if anyone is moving.

If someone moves, they are out of the game and help the leader to look for moving statues.

The last person remaining in the game is the winner.

INDOOR TRACK

What you need: Speed and versatility

Ideally played: Indoors

HOW TO PLAY:

Indoor track is a series of races, but instead of running them, players crawl, belly crawl, back crawl, and roll. Players clear a space from a good size room in the house and select a start and finish line. Races are conducted the same way as running races, "On your mark, get set, GO!" Players take off and the first across the finish line is the winner. Make sure that this one is played in a room without any dangerous obstacles, especially for the rolling version.

To make it really fun, have a grand prix event, with players crawling out of the living room, down the hall, through the kitchen and back into the living room.

The first player to do three laps of the course is the winner! There is no end to the variety of races that can be run, just adapt it for indoors with crawling.

INDOOR CRAZY GOLF

What you need: A play set of golf clubs and plastic golf balls

Ideally played: Indoors

HOW TO PLAY:

This is a tremendously fun game to play! Players get together and design a course, using as many rooms of the house as possible. If you live in a two or three story house, play should begin on the top floor and work down - it's not easy to chip up a flight of stairs!

Each room in the house used is one hole and players determine how many shots makes par for each room. For example, if you think that it's possible to get the ball in the hole in three shots, then you should make that hole a 3-par hole. If a player makes it in three shots she gets "0" for that hole. If she makes it in two shots, then she gets "-1". If she makes it in four shots, then she gets "+1" for the hole.

Make the holes as challenging as possible by putting obstacles in front of them. You can use plastic cups as holes or even masking tape to create a "hole" in the floor. If using masking tape, make the holes slightly larger as it's more difficult to land the ball inside without any edges. The player who finishes the course with the lowest score wins!

MARCO POLO (INDOOR VERSION)

What you need: A blindfold and an open space

Ideally played: Indoors

HOW TO PLAY:

This is an indoor version of the all-time-great swimming pool game. One player is selected to be "IT" and is blindfolded in the middle of the room, on his knees. The other players quietly scatter themselves around the room, on their knees. Play starts with "IT" calling out "MARCO!" Every time that "IT" says "MARCO", the other players have to respond with "POLO!"

The object is for "IT" to find the players by the sound of their voice and tag them. The players can move around the play area as much as they want, but must be careful to do it quietly so that "IT" doesn't hear them. Players can only move around by walking on their knees, and cannot use their hands in any way. When a player is tagged, she is out of the game and must leave the playing area.

The last player remaining is the winner.

PIN-THE-TAIL-ON-THE-MONKEY

What you need: A good drawing, a paper tail and a piece of blue tack

Ideally played: Indoors

HOW TO PLAY:

This is the same as Pin-the-tail-on-the-donkey, except that players decide what they want to pin the tail onto and draw it first. Some players like to pin the tail on the daddy, and draw a picture of their dad. Other players might want to pin the tail on the dinosaur. Whatever the players decide to use, they draw and color in the picture and a corresponding tail. Cut the picture and tail out and put blue tack (or white tack) on the back of the tail. Tape the picture to a wall and line players up about five feet away from it.

Players select an order of play, and each player is blindfolded on their turn, spun around five or ten times, pointed in the right direction and let go with the tail in their hands.

The object of the game is to stick the tail as close as possible to where it is supposed to go on the picture. This game is more fun the further away players get the tail!

INDOOR BASKETBALL or WAD BALL

What you need: A wastepaper basket and some crumpled paper

Ideally played: Indoors

HOW TO PLAY:

There are as many versions of this game as in standard basketball. A wastepaper basket is placed at one end of the room. Players can play one-on-one, two-on-two, foul shot competition, or h-o-r-s-e. The best versions for indoors are foul shot and h-o-r-s-e. For foul shot competitions, players each get ten shots from a specified distance. Players take shots with a piece of crumpled paper. The player with the most points at the end wins.

For h-o-r-s-e, the rules are the same as the outdoor version. A player invents a shot (bank off the wall). If she makes it, each player after her has to make the same shot. If they miss the shot, then they get a letter. A player is out of the game when they receive the same amount of letters as the name of the game. For h-o-r-s-e, a player has five chances. For p-i-g, they have only three chances. If the player inventing the shot misses, he loses his turn, but doesn't get a letter to his name.

The last player remaining in the game is the winner!

MORE

SPIRIT AND ADVENTURE

Nothing is as vast as our imagination. As we get older however, responsibilities and commitments cast a fog on our memory of how fun it was to play. Sure; we still golf, swim, play tennis, go to the gym, walk, jog and bicycle. But many of us do it more as a form of exercise than adventure now. Unfortunately, today's children are more apt to pick up a handheld video game than they are to rally together a group of friends to start a game of Kick the Can.

I was fortunate enough to be borne to parents who believed that childhood was precious. Even when I wanted to work as a young boy, my parents told me not to rush into it - that I'd be working the rest of my life. They supported my role in life and allowed me to be a child; to climb trees, ride bikes, build forts, go exploring, and play with my friends.

Play teaches us so much. It strengthens our mental, physical and social skills.

In play, we learn how to resolve conflict through compromise: the simplicity of "do-over" as a method of balancing two opposing opinions during play could be a lesson for many corporate and political quarrels.

In play, we learn how to be fair: the process of selecting "IT" is based on pure objectivity.

In play, we learn how to be tolerant: no player is too small, too slow or too awkward to be included in the game.

In play, we learn to adapt: rules are introduced as needed to ensure an even playing field or to increase the challenge for skilled players.

In play, we learn teamwork: making a human chain in jail to give our remaining teammates a better chance to free us demonstrates our unity.

In play, we learn to trust:
there is no greater ally than your playing partner.

In play, we learn to take chances:
it is possible to make it to the other side if I run now.

In play, we learn to laugh and not take ourselves too seriously:
it's just a game after all.

We also allow our bodies to move and stretch and flex in a natural way. Play doesn't feel like exercise. It's just something that we choose to do because it is fun.

As children, we long for adventure. Even when there aren't other children around to play with, we seek it. We ride bikes, build forts, explore, watch bugs, climb trees, bounce balls off a wall, go roller skating, skateboarding and sledding. We are active as children, or at least we used to be.

Unfortunately, many children today are seduced, like us, by the technology that we have created over the years. The colorful, interactive graphics of computer generated games are seductive – and addictive. Play has changed over the years. Even active play these days is different than it used to be. Children today are shuttled back and forth, to and from organized, structured activities. There are coaches, uniforms, instructions, skill assessments, fees and commitments in modern play. Houses are no longer connected by the footprints of children, and many neighborhoods are quiet today. Children no longer have to invent games; they just have to participate in them. They don't make the rules, they abide by them. They don't pick the teams, they join them.

I hope that this book revives the magic of active neighborhood play. I hope that it encourages parents to let their children make the rules and explore the possibilities. I hope that it inspires communities to get loud and connected again. And I hope that it helps some of my old gang and other veterans of play to see through the fog that has descended over the years, so that they can remember how fun life used to be.

Tag, YOU'RE IT!

GLOSSARY